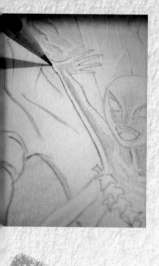

CREATING FANTASY ART
How To Draw
WEIRD
Fantasy Art

STEVE BEAUMONT

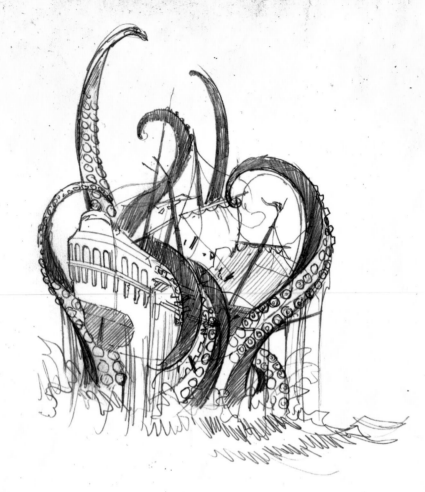

Published in 2018 by
The Rosen Publishing Group, Inc.
29 East 21st Street
New York, NY 10010

Library of Congress Cataloging-in-Publication Data

Names: Beaumont, Steve, author.
Title: How to draw weird fantasy art / Steve Beaumont.
Description: New York : Rosen, 2018. | Series: Creating fantasy art | Includes bibliographical references and index. | Audience: 7–12.
Identifiers: LCCN 2017005746| ISBN 9781508175957 (pbk.) | ISBN 9781508175940 (library bound) | ISBN 9781508175919 (6 pack)
Subjects: LCSH: Fantasy in art—Juvenile literature. | Drawing—Technique—Juvenile literature.
Classification: LCC NC825.F25 B4325 2018 | DDC 700/.415—dc23
LC record available at https://lccn.loc.gov/2017005746

Manufactured in the United States of America

All illustrations are original. Credits for additional images: Shutterstock: 19, 20, 28

CONTENTS

ROCK 'N' ROLL VAMPIRE

THE ENCHANTED

KRAKEN

INTRODUCTION

What is it about fantasy art that so many find appealing? Is it that it covers so many different genres, from horror and science fiction to swashbuckling, swords and sorcery? Is it that it offers the opportunity to engage with extraordinary characters and creatures in extraordinary worlds? Is it because there are no barriers and that anything is possible? The answer is that it is all of these things, and every individual enjoys different aspects of the genre. In this book we will explore a small collection of some of those characters and the worlds they inhabit and in the process create some exciting fantasy art.

I have had a life-long love affair with comics, books and films dealing with themes of fantasy. As a child, I enjoyed nothing more than reading DC Comics' *Batman* series drawn by Dick Sprang, the first artist to inspire me to produce a piece of fantasy art. Later, motivation was provided by Jack Kirby and Frank Frazetta's art. In my teenage years, Frazetta's work opened up all kinds of possibilities for fantasy drawings, based upon and inspired by my favorite tv shows and films, including *Doctor Who*, *The Outer Limits*, *The Twilight Zone*, *Frankenstein* and *Creature from the Black Lagoon*.

I have been professionally providing illustration, concept art, storyboards and (occasionally) comic-book art for the past 20 years or so. I have had no professional tutoring: everything I have learned has been self-taught, proving that anyone, with practice, can produce fantastic and fantastical art. What I will be passing on to you within the pages of this book are some of the techniques and approaches I have developed, either by accident or by watching other artists at work, over my professional career.

I also teach a 'how to draw fantasy art' class and this book incorporates some of the themes and tutorials used there. It is a companion book, if you like. During the years the class has been running, I have successfully enabled a number of students to compile a portfolio of work, which they showed to talent scouts at comic conventions and eventually led to them getting commissions from Marvel Comics. What I will be showing you in the following pages are easy-to-follow steps that will guide you through the process of producing a piece of fantasy art. I have not gone into every minute detail and this is because, as I keep telling my students, I do not want to encourage you to copy my style and exactly how I draw as if it were the only way, as we all have to find our own path forward.

This book is not aimed at the professional or semi-professional artist, it is more for those (the amateur, if you like) who enjoy drawing and are fans of fantasy art and are looking for some tips and ideas that will enable them to take their drawings skills a stage further. I thought it would also be helpful to document any changes I thought of as I went along. Unlike drawings I produce for a client, which are meticulously planned and go through various stages of development, I have approached these artworks as I would any drawing I am producing just for myself – complete with mistakes, experiments and last-minute revisions. I have included these thoughts and alterations in the hope that they will encourage you constantly to seek to improve your work. Remember, it's vital not to worry too much about making mistakes – instead, keep the drawings you are not happy with to remind you what not to do next time.

When I was having fun drawing as a child, I mostly drew from comic books and from what I had seen on tv or at the movies. Basically, I drew what pleased me and what I was interested in, and this is true of most fantasy artists. For instance, Frank Frazetta is a sports fan and, from what I have read, something of an athlete, and this is evident in his work. Adi Granov has a love of automobiles, aircraft and machinery and these are strong features in his drawings. Claire Wendling clearly has a love, understanding and passion for wildlife and nature. They draw what they are passionate about and this makes them better artists, in my opinion.

Personally, I love horror and sci-fi movies and comics and 70 percent of my daily work is related to these themes. I enjoy working with this subject matter and I hope you find drawing it as fun and exciting as I do and that it will encourage you to become a better artist.

Have fun!

Steve Beaumont

The prehistoric beast in *Creature from the Black Lagoon*, 1954

Figure Drawing

Figure drawing can be a huge stumbling block for many beginners and even for some people who have been drawing for a while. When it comes to drawing dragons or other beasts there often appears to be no problem at all, but when a well-balanced figure drawing is required, issues can arise. In the next pages I offer some of the approaches to figure drawing that have helped my students gain more confidence. This section is intended to give a basic overview of the techniques so that they can be applied assuredly to imaginative drawings.

BASIC ANATOMY

Humans come in all shapes and sizes and with all kinds of variations that make each one unique, but for the purpose of getting started on producing a balanced and well-proportioned figure, let's look at the basic, muscular, human form. As a rough guide, the adult human form is about seven-and-a-half heads tall. However, it is common practice to exaggerate the proportions of fantasy characters, and the imagined figure is more usually eight-and-three-quarters heads tall, whether it is male or female (Figure 1). I, as well as my students, have found it helpful to have a rough knowledge of the skeletal structure of our bodies. I can draw a figure better if I understand how it should look and how it works, otherwise I am merely guessing and filling in the vague areas using incomplete information, which will be evident in the end result. The human skeleton comprises about 206 bones, some of which are labelled in Figure 2.

Memorizing the names for each and every bone is not essential for successful figure drawing, but it is helpful to be familiar with the names, proportions and joint structures of ones that are most important for drawing the human form. It would take far too long to draw a complete skeleton every time you wanted to draw a figure and, moreover, it is not necessary. Instead, you can simply break down the skeleton into some basic, manageable shapes or lines and this should enable you to achieve some pleasing results.

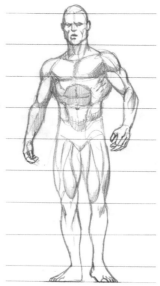

Figure 1

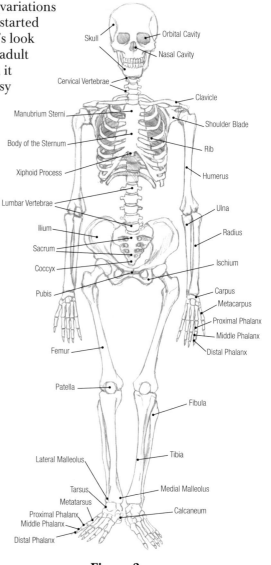

Figure 2 labels: Skull, Orbital Cavity, Nasal Cavity, Cervical Vertebrae, Clavicle, Manubrium Sterni, Shoulder Blade, Body of the Sternum, Rib, Xiphoid Process, Humerus, Lumbar Vertebrae, Ulna, Ilium, Radius, Sacrum, Ischium, Coccyx, Pubis, Carpus, Metacarpus, Proximal Phalanx, Middle Phalanx, Distal Phalanx, Femur, Patella, Fibula, Lateral Malleolus, Tibia, Tarsus, Medial Malleolus, Metatarsus, Calcaneum, Proximal Phalanx, Middle Phalanx, Distal Phalanx

Figure 2

BREAKING DOWN THE FIGURE

My students have achieved good results with three approaches to figure drawing. Some students responded well to stripping down the skeleton to a simplified stick form as shown in Figure 1, while others had more success using construction shapes – an assortment of ovals, cylinders and spheres – to construct a figure, as shown in Figure 2. I personally go about figure drawing by loosely sketching the form and feeling my way around the shape as I go along, as shown in Figure 3, and some students have also found using this approach useful. Whichever method you choose, you should be able to arrive at a completed figure, as shown in Figure 4.

With all these methods, the main points to keep in mind are the size of the head in relation to the body (page 6, Figure 1) and the length and position of the arms and legs. The arms can be divided into two roughly equal lengths. In reality, the upper leg (thigh) is generally longer than the lower leg (shin and calf area). However, when creating fantasy art, I tend to draw them both about

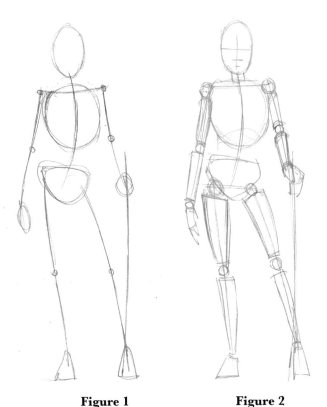

Figure 1   **Figure 2**

the same length, but with the upper leg wider and thicker-set than the lower leg. The torso can be put together using an oval (I sometimes draw a shape that resembles a rib cage, as in Figure 3) for the rib cage and a shape resembling a pair of briefs for the pelvis.

It is good practice to study yourself in the mirror – preferably a full-length one – to become aware of how certain poses affect parts of the body. For example, try standing with both legs straight with your bodyweight centered over them, then transfer your bodyweight to just one leg. Notice the effect this movement has on the other leg. What has happened to the stance? What differences do you notice? Has the shift of weight affected other parts of the body, such as the pelvis, your shoulders or the curve of your back and spine? What about the angle of your head? Recreating what you see in the mirror in your figure drawing will make the artwork that much more convincing. (You could take a photo of your reflection in a certain stance to refer to while you are drawing.)

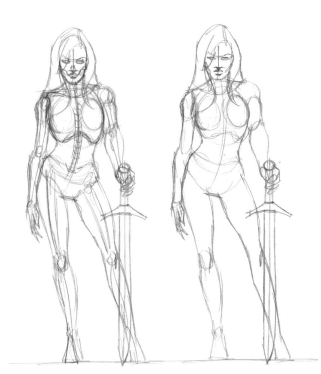

Figure 3   **Figure 4**

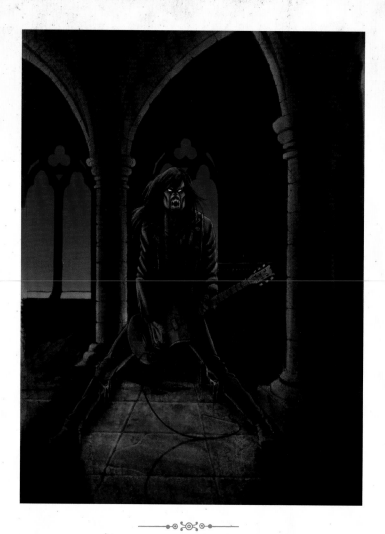

---•◦⟨⟩◦•---

Rock 'n' Roll Vampire

---•◦⟨⟩◦•---

This drawing was inspired by movies I've seen that show undead rock musicians. These images have stuck with me over the years. This artwork was produced on 300gsm cartridge paper, using a combination of a Palomino Blackwing 602 pencil and a HB Staedtler pencil, then colored in Photoshop. It can also be produced as a monochrome pencil or ink drawing.

Figure 1

Figure 2

I began by producing some rough sketches of rock/metal guitarists (Figures 1 and 2). Initially the character I envisaged was based on Norwegian black metal guitarists with a demonic twist. I knew what setting I wanted, but wasn't sure of the pose. These sketches helped me see what did and didn't work. At the end of the process I decided that, although I really liked them, these drawings were moving away from my original idea, so I filed them away for use on another piece and started again.

This time I decided to go for more of a 1980s goth/punk feel, playing down the drama of the guitar shapes and making the instrument more low-key (Figure 3). Although I really like over-the-top, dramatic, in-your-face visuals, I also like more subtle imagery where the lighting and space set the tone as much as the figure.

Figure 3

STEP 1

Begin to plot the drawing using the vaulting and Gothic window in the background to frame the figure. In order to get the detail correct for a more realistic setting, it is important to source some reference materials, either by sitting and producing rough sketches in a small pocket-sized sketchbook (Figure 4) or by taking or looking up photos (Figures 5 and 6). Keep this reference material in folders, both real and virtual, and over time you will build up an archive of invaluable information and inspiration that can be accessed quickly and easily.

Figure 4

Figure 5

Figure 6

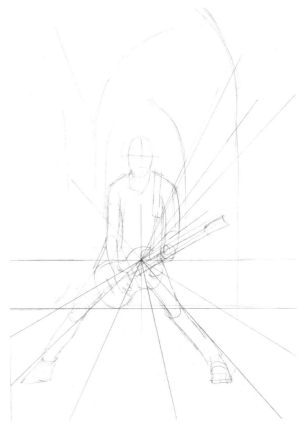

STEP 2

To plot the layout correctly, take time to draw some perspective lines, which will enable you to gauge the position of the pillars and the size and angles of the flagstones on the floor.

STEP 3

Referring to the photos of Gothic architecture, begin to apply details to the pillars and vaulting. Since this will be a dark environment you need only be concerned with the basic structural details. Do some research and choose equipment you like the look of, then use it to help you draw the guitar and amplifier. Having spent a lot of time attending rock concerts I am very familiar with sound equipment as well as guitars. I was going to model the guitar on a Fender Stratocaster, but in the end I based it on a Mosrite guitar, simply because the shape appealed to me at the time. It could also easily have been a flying V-shaped Ibanez guitar. The amp is based on a Marshall amplifier and the skull and crossbones image on the front is a nod to Gothic rock band Avenged Sevenfold.

STEP 4

Once the working drawing is complete, trace it on to a clean sheet of cartridge paper using a lightbox.

STEP 5

Begin to establish the darker, blacker areas using a pencil (I used a Palamino Blackwing 602), applying heavier pencil work in the background and lighter tones to the pillar in the foreground.

STEP 6

Blend the pencil work to a smoother finish using a blending stump rather than a piece of tissue, so that you can be really accurate.

STEP 7

Using a Staedtler HB pencil, apply some mid-range tones to the vaulting and pillars. Pay attention to where the light source is coming from and position the highlights appropriately.

STEP 8

Using a sharp Staedtler HB pencil, add some detail to the lighter areas of stonework that will be more visible and add shading to the underside of the stonework. Even though the coloring and lighting will obscure most of the details, they will add texture.

STEP 9

Still using a Staedtler HB pencil, apply lighter tones and texture to the flooring by lightly running the flat end of the lead across the surface of the paper.

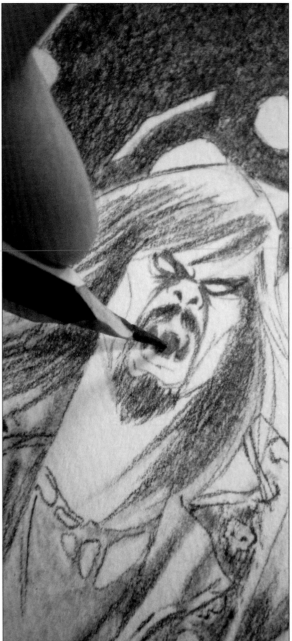

STEP 10

Again, using a sharp HB pencil, tighten up the finer details of the figure, paying special attention to the hair and face. Little details such as the holes in the t-shirt and the skull decoration on the guitar strap give character to the figure. Although these are small details and not immediately noticeable, they provide important information and add interest.

STEP II

Once all the pencil work is finished, sit back and assess the drawing. Are more highlights required? Does the line-work need blending more? I did some additional blending on the stone floor using a blending stump and added some subtle highlights to the stonework, pillars and figure using the sharp end of an eraser.

At this stage you could stop, since the pencil drawing is now complete. Alternatively, you could ink the drawing in black ink, color it using markers, or do as I did and scan the image and color it using Photoshop.

The rough color work in Figure 7 was created early on, after I produced the thumbnail sketch. I scanned the image, imported it into Photoshop and created a color scheme. At the time I thought the colors worked, but when I looked at it again I realized that the tones were not correct for giving the impression of the setting sun seen through the window. When I came to produce the final image I decided to keep the color palette simple, as I do for most illustrations.

Figure 7

STEP 12

Once you have imported the final pencil illustration into Photoshop, create a base color layer of pale orange by using the Fill option on a low opacity, on the Multiply setting. All the brushwork here was done using a single brush I created by scanning a pencil rubbing. You may have other brushes that better suit the way you work – try things out and have fun experimenting.

STEP 13

Create a new layer, set to Multiply, and use a brush to add a pale olive green to the shadowed areas of stonework. Notice how this immediately changes the atmosphere of the piece.

STEP 14

Continue to build up tonal work on the stone with separate layers of pale olive and warm grey, set to Multiply, until you achieve a range of subtle tones.

STEP 15

Color the sky, seen through the window, using three layers. The first layer is orange, the second is red and the third is a darker red with a hint of black, which I used for the darker upper tone. All layers should be set to Multiply.

STEP 16

To finish off the interior of the church, apply a few layers of orange. I adjusted the opacity of the first layer to create the right tone to blend with the olive colors underneath. Then I built up the darker, warmer tones with deeper shades of orange, the last of which had a percentage of grey in it.

STEP 17

Once you are happy with the setting, focus on the figure. Strengthen the shadows using a dark warm grey and refine the features of the face. Add details to the guitar. Finally, add bloodstains and spatters around the vampire's mouth and clothing and on the guitar.

THE ENCHANTED

Fantasy films are often a rich source of inspiration, and this drawing pays homage to characters created by director Guillermo del Toro. I didn't want to draw an exact re-creation of the characters I have seen, so I purposely relied solely on my memory rather than looking at clips. This makes sure that there are some differences between his faun and fairies and the ones in this exercise.

Figure 1

Figure 2

I started by creating some rough thumbnail sketches exploring variations on a theme. In Figure 1, I included a magic symbol behind the faun, which framed the subject. Initially I liked this approach, but then I thought it was too contrived, so I placed the faun and the fairy in an archway covered in ivy (Figure 2). I preferred the uncluttered layout and decided to use this arrangement.

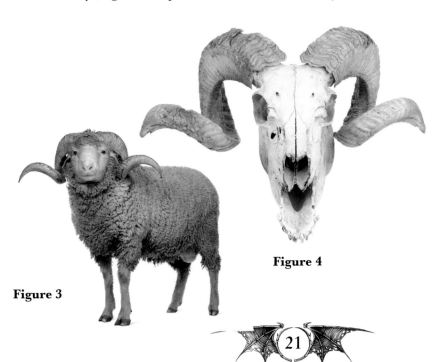

Figure 4

Figure 3

Fauns are generally depicted as half human and half goat. As usual, you need to source some reference material, such as a photo of a sheep or goat (Figure 3) and some horns (Figure 4), so you can get a feel for the shape and detail of the objects. Having studied real objects you can then adapt them for fantasy art using a bit of artistic licence.

Before I began the final piece of artwork, I wanted to make sure that I was happy with the faces of the faun and the fairy. Although I liked the middle and bottom sketches of the faun (Figure 6 and Figure 7), I felt they looked a bit too evil, so I decided to use the top sketch (Figure 5).

I also explored a variety of ideas for the design of the fairy (Figure 8) before deciding on the final design. I chose Figure 9.

Figure 5

Figure 6

Figure 7

Figure 8

Figure 9

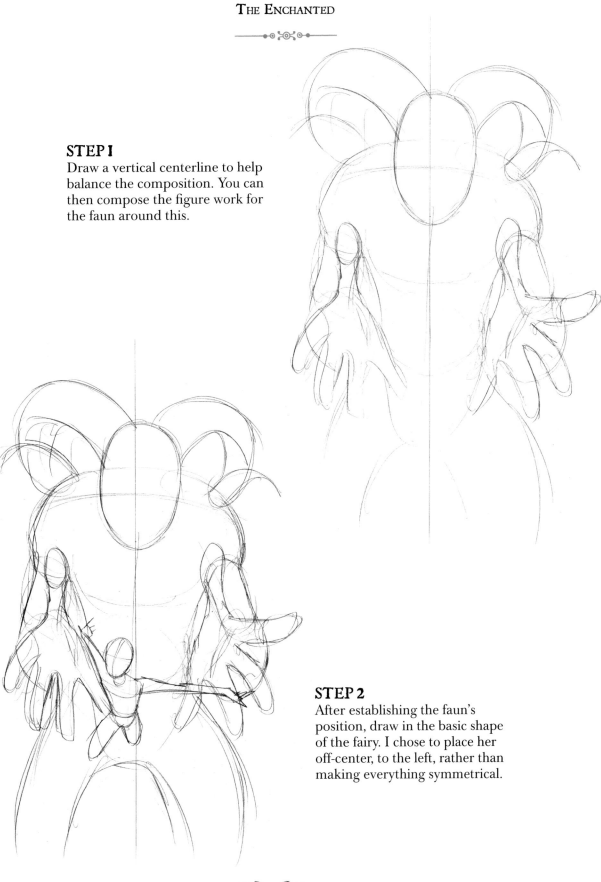

STEP 1
Draw a vertical centerline to help balance the composition. You can then compose the figure work for the faun around this.

STEP 2
After establishing the faun's position, draw in the basic shape of the fairy. I chose to place her off-center, to the left, rather than making everything symmetrical.

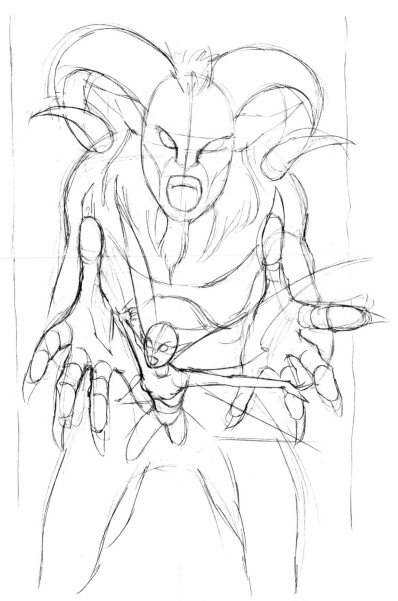

STEP 3

Once you have established the positions of the figures, focus on the outer surrounding detail, which in this case will be a stone arch covered in ivy. I was familiar enough with ivy to be able to draw a believable representation, but it helps to have a visual reference (Figure 10). This shows that an ivy leaf consists of three or five points, and some appear to be almost triangular, so a mixture of all three leaf shapes would create authentic foliage.

Figure 10

STEP 4
Keep the leaf shapes simple and gradually cover the stone pillars,
trying to make the foliage appear to grow naturally upwards.

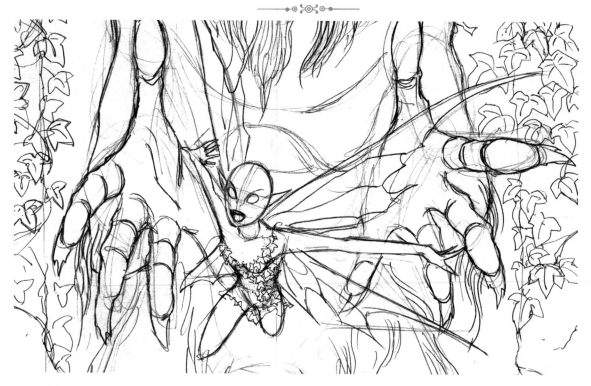

STEP 5

You can now consider the characters' costumes. Rather than leaving the fairy naked, I thought it might be nice to continue the ivy theme and create a kind of short ivy dress. The leaves here are a lot smaller than those climbing the stone archway.

STEP 6

Once all the line work has been established, add shading to the background with a B pencil. I used an HB towards the bottom of the page for a lighter tone as I knew I would be erasing some of it to form highlights, and it is easier to erase HB lead.

STEP 7
You can now apply mid-range tones to the stone wall,
the faun's legs and the outer edges of the arms.

STEP 9

You can now carefully blend the shaded areas of the faun. You may prefer to use a blending stump for the smaller areas.

STEP 8

Using a blending stump or tissue paper, blend the mid-range pencil work. I purposely went over the ivy while blending to give the leaves some tone. I find this is achieved more successfully using tissue paper rather than a blending stump, though you may prefer the effect provided by the stump. Leave plenty of light around the central area where the fairy is positioned, as this will be the main light source.

STEP 10

Apply a dark shadow to the ivy. The shadow would be cast by the central light source, so the direction of the shadow will change depending on where the ivy is in relation to the light. The ivy leaves at the top left of the page will cast a shadow to the far top left, whereas those at the bottom left will cast a shadow to the far bottom left.

STEP 11

Here you can see that the shadow lifts the ivy away from the stone.
You should check the shading at this stage, before adding highlights.

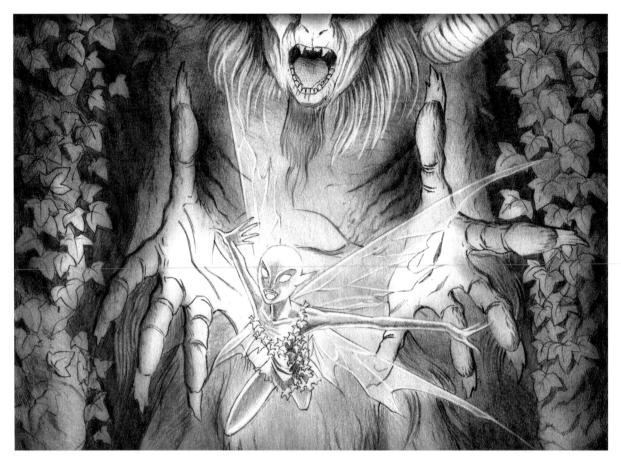

STEP 12

It is now time to apply highlights to the areas that are nearest the light source, including the faun's face, hair (Figure 11) and hands; the ivy nearest the light source (Figure 12); and the veins in the fairy's wings. This not only brightens up the drawing but also creates a sense of depth.

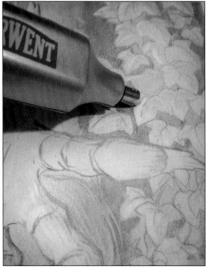

Figure 11

Figure 12

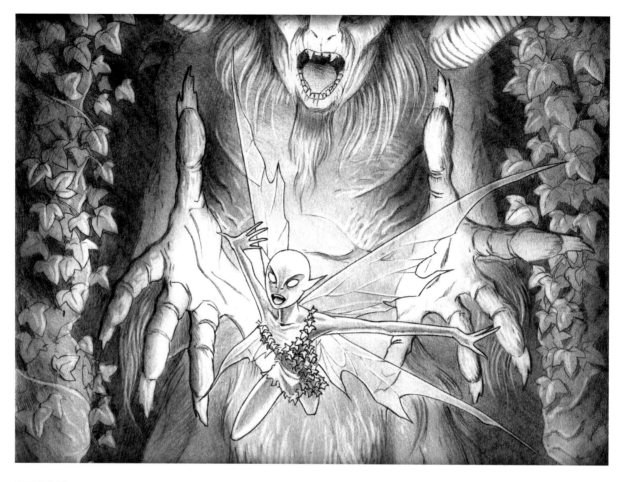

STEP 13

After applying the highlights, the drawing needs to be tidied up. Draw a thin, crisp line around the body of the faun and the fairy (Figure 13), paying particular attention to the wings (Figure 14). Notice how the thin line work adds strength and clarity to the drawing.

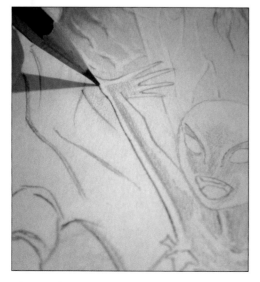

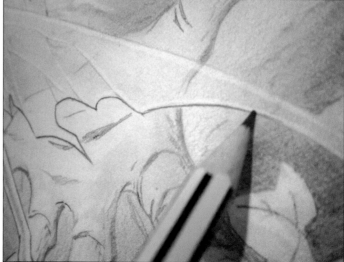

Figure 13

Figure 14

STEP 14

The final step is to add rays of light shooting from between the hands of the faun, creating a fantastical light source for the image. This was achieved using the round-edged stump of a plastic eraser. A putty rubber can also be used.

The final drawing can be seen on the opposite page.

KRAKEN

I have long enjoyed watching movies that feature giant, tentacled marine creatures, such as *20,000 Leagues Under the Sea*, *It Came From Beneath the Sea* and *Clash of the Titans*. I am an unashamed fan of all Walt Disney's *Pirates of the Caribbean* movies, but my favorite is *Pirates of the Caribbean: Dead Man's Chest*, which features the mighty sea monster, Kraken. The above painting was inspired by a scene in which the Kraken takes down the ship the "Black Pearl."

The painting was produced using Winsor & Newton gouache on cold-pressed 300gsm Arches Aquarelle Watercolor Paper.

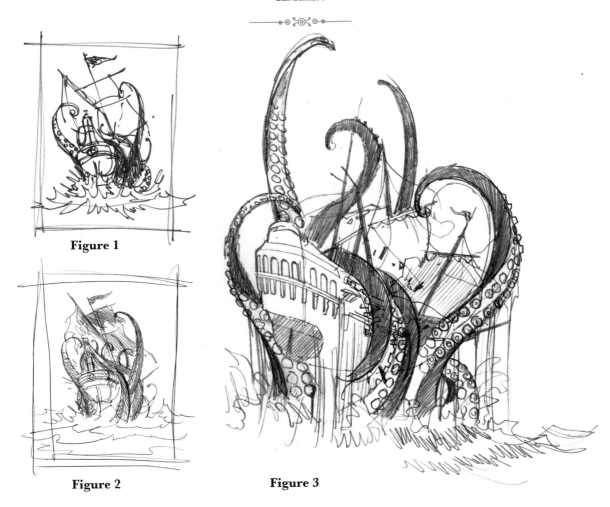

Figure 1

Figure 2

Figure 3

As usual, I started by drawing some rough thumbnail sketches to work out the position of the boat and how the tentacles should wrap around it. These early ideas are shown in Figures 1–3, and you can see the progression of the level of detail drawn and the different angles I tried out. I decided to use the set-up shown in Figure 2 and went on to color the image using markers (Figures 4 and 5) in order to establish the color scheme before I started painting.

Figure 4

Figure 5

Before drawing the ship in the grip of the Kraken, I produced a quick sketch (Figure 6) to work out the shape of the ship accurately, ensuring that all the basic components were present and in the correct place. Sourcing reference material for unfamiliar subjects such as ships is always a good idea, particularly when you want them to look of a period, in which case the shape and detailing are especially important.

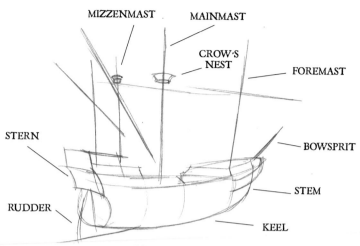

Figure 6

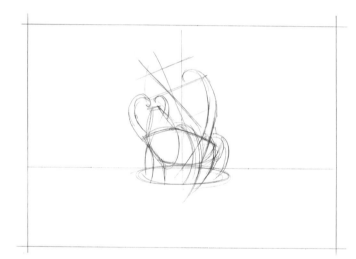

STEP 1

When you are going to paint on watercolor paper it is worth drawing the image first on standard paper (I used A3-size paper) and then lightly tracing the working drawing on to the watercolor paper. This prevents the watercolor paper becoming marked with workings out that then need to be erased, and makes for a much better end result.

Start by marking the horizon and plotting the image around a center line. At this stage I was still undecided about whether to tilt the ship up or down. In the end I decided to show the ship being crushed by the Kraken's tentacles, which means that it would appear to be angled up and leaning to the left. I also drew in the position and action of the tentacles.

STEP 2

Add more details to the ship, trying to make them as accurate as possible. Roughly draw in the clouds and waves, arranging them so that they lead the eye towards the center of the painting, where the action is taking place.

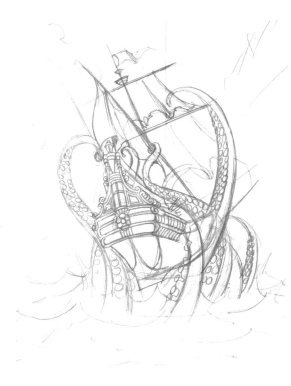

STEP 3

Refine the decorative detail on the ship's stern and on the tentacles. This ship is the result of a combination of reference sources, including some old books about sailing ships I have collected. However, by the time I finished it I realized the artwork was as much a homage to Frank Frazetta's painting "The Galleon" as anything else. Discoveries like this are part of the fun of fantasy art.

STEP 4

Shade the clouds and the rear of the ship to establish the areas that will have the darkest tones. The waves here are exaggerated, but when I drew smaller ones the image looked rather tame, so I went for bigger, more dramatic waves to create the appearance of a great disturbance in the sea.

Once you are happy with the working drawing, trace it on to a sheet of watercolor paper using a lightbox. It is a good idea to stretch the watercolor paper first by laying it flat in a bath or sink of water and soaking it for 10–15 minutes, ensuring it is completely saturated. Lift it out and allow the excess water to drip off, then tape it flat to a clean, level board or desk with brown paper gumstrip and leave to dry. By saturating and then drying the paper before you add watercolors, you avoid running the risk of the paper buckling when you use numerous washes of paint.

When the paper is ready, angle the board or desk so that when you apply washes of color the paint will flow downwards. I use an adjustable drawing desk, but if you do not own one you could try using more affordable portable easels or desk easels, which are available at most art and craft stores.

Once the paper is prepared and ready, assemble the paints you need to complete the art. I have kept to a simple palette, using the following tones of blue, yellow and green: Sky Blue, Cobalt Blue, Winsor Blue, Prussian Blue, Cadmium Yellow, Yellow Ochre, Raw Sienna, Olive Green, Sepia and Jet Black.

STEP 5

Apply a first wash of very watered down Cadmium Yellow Pale. I used a size 12 Winsor & Newton sable brush.

STEP 6

While the yellow wash is still wet, apply a wash of Sky Blue, allowing the blue to run into the yellow to create a soft blending effect between the colors.

STEP 7

Build up the strength of color in the clouds. I used Winsor Blue and Prussian Blue mixed with a very small amount of Jet Black. The Winsor Blue was applied as a concentrated wash, while the consistency of the Prussian Blue mixed with Jet Black was slightly thicker than a wash, but still wet enough to allow color spread.

STEP 8

Allow the first washes to dry, then apply layers of Cadmium Yellow, Yellow Ochre and Raw Sienna to the body of the ship. Build up the color of the tentacles using washes of Olive Green and Sepia, both with just a hint of Jet Black. Add washes of Olive Green and Sepia to the ship's sails.

Figure 7

STEP 9

Apply thicker, less liquid layers of Prussian Blue and Jet Black to the clouds, using a dry brush effect to break up the color and create texture (Figure 7). All brush strokes should be directed towards the center of the image, so that they surround the action. I used a size 8 flat shader brush.

STEP II

Add thicker layers of Olive Green mixed with Sepia and Jet Black to build up the solid, darker tones of the tentacles to give them more presence. I applied darker mixes to the very top and round the inside and outer edges of the suckers to create a sense of shape and depth. I used a size 8 flat shader and a size 3 sable brush for the finer work on the tentacles.

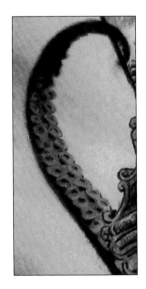

STEP 10

Add thicker washes of Olive Green mixed with a tiny amount of Jet Black to the sails, applying darker tones to the top of the sails.

STEP 12

Using a size 8 flat shader and a size 1 flat shader, apply more concentrated layers of Cobalt Blue and Prussian Blue, both mixed with a little Jet Black, to the waves. You are aiming to add just enough black paint to darken each tone of blue. The waves should become progressively darker towards the outer areas of the painting.

With a size 8 flat shader and thin pastes of Olive Green and Sepia, create a dry brush effect on the stern, to give some texture. Use darker tones of Sepia and Jet Black to highlight the detail on the stern, rudder and underside of the ship.

STEP 13

Using undiluted Permanent White, apply a dry brush effect
to the surf of the waves and the base of the ship to create the
illusion that the ship is being lifted out of the sea.

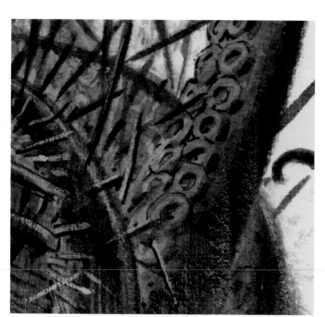

STEP 14

For the final touches, use a size 1 brush to apply Jet Black to the sails, tentacles and finer details of the ship to give them more strength. Use undiluted Permanent White and a fine brush to highlight details on the stern and the broken timbers.

STEP 15

Apply one last coat of black to the clouds and parts of the waves to give them more strength. This creates a dark, framing effect, drawing the eye to the center of the image.

SKETCHBOOK

I often stress the importance of keeping sketchbooks to my students. They can be used for any kind of drawing – from observational sketches or the exploration of ideas to testing out new materials (pens, pencils, paints, etc.) or just doodling for the fun of it. All these activities help to develop drawing skills and, as with most things, the more you practice, the better you become.

   Professional artists fill dozens of sketchbooks. The rough workings of some, including Frank Frazetta, Jeffrey Jones and Claire Wendling, have been turned into high-end art books that showcase their creative processes. The seeds of some of your best ideas may be doodled in a sketchbook. Ideas flow uninhibited when you are not feeling too precious about your drawing and you may often experience a breakthrough in this way.

GLOSSARY

anatomy The body structure of humans and animals.

faun A creature that is half human and half goat.

foliage Leafy plants.

genre A style of film, art, music or literature.

Gothic A style of architecture.

gouache Paint with a glue-like texture.

homage Something created as a tribute to someone else's work.

lightbox A flat box with a translucent top and light inside, used by artists to help when tracing pictures.

original New work created by a specific artist.

perspective lines Guidelines drawn on paper before an artist starts work, to help accurately create depth in a picture.

pose The way that a person stands.

science fiction A genre that uses themes of imagined futuristic science and technology.

tentacle A flexible limb of some animals.

vaulting Decorations on a roof that is made from a series of arches.

FURTHER INFORMATION

Chris Riddell's Doodle-a-Day by Chris Riddell (Macmillan Children's Books, 2015)

Draw and Write Your Own Comics by Louie Stowell (Usborne Publishing, 2014)

Drawing Fantasy Creatures by Aaron Sautter (Capstone Press, 2016)

Drawing Manga: Step-by-Step by Ben Krefta (Arcturus Publishing, 2013)

Drawing Wizards, Witches and Warlocks by Christ Hart
    (Sixth and Spring Books, 2009)

How to Draw Fantasy Art by Mark Bergin (PowerKids Press, 2011)

Terry Pratchett's Discworld Colouring Book by Paul Kidby (Gollancz, 2016)

INDEX